# *Dedication*

*To everyday heroes whose efforts help defeat evil.*

# CONTENTS

| | | |
|---|---|---|
| I. | Family trees and photo | 3,4,5 |
| II. | Tante Isa's military ID | 6 |
| III. | Acknowledgements | 7 |
| IV. | Prologue | 8 |
| V. | My recollections from my mother's point of view | 9,10 |
| VI. | Map of Europe 1940 | 11 |
| VII. | Photo collage | 12 |
| VIII. | Resistance groups | 13,14 |
| IX. | TRANSLATIONS: | 15-21 |

    A. I have taken the liberty to summarize how Tante Isa's Resistance participation evolved, then the path of her detentions, and a record of her correspondence with her brothers based on the notes given to me by my cousin Juliette Renard.

    B. With some commentary of my own, I have given a fairly rigid translation of the transcripts of Tante Isa's trial and sentencing based on records sent to me by my cousin Isabelle Renard and then further supported and expanded by the transcripts received from the Belgian War Archives "Cega Soma."

Items included in this section are:
- #1. Isabelle Godenne's background introduced at her trial, April 17, 1943 by the Luftwaffe Tribunal
- #2. Summary of her crime against the German Reich
- #3. Description of the situation with presumed Allied Pilot #1
- #4. Description of the situation with presumed Allied Pilot #2
- #5. Luftwaffe Tribunal's accusation, Tante Isa's defense
- #6. The verdicts and sentencing
- #7. Her Prisons and transfers until Waldheim Prison, Germany

| | | |
|---|---|---|
| X. | "The Women in Waldheim Prison", by Gabriele Hackl | 22, 23 |
| XI. | Tante Isa's Liberation May 7, 1945 | 23, 24, 25 |
| XII. | Forever a Devout Catholic | 26 |
| XIII. | Artifacts and Memorabilia | 27, 28, 29 |
| XIV. | Tante Isa's small album of her 16 day journey home | 30 |
| XV. | Map of Europe during WWII showing her journey | 31 |
| XVI. | Life after Liberation, excerpts taken from Caroline Moorehead's book, **A Train In Winter** | 32,33 |
| XVII. | 1982 Belgian newspapers death announcement about Tante Isa given to me by Isabelle Renard, translated into English | 34 |
| XVIII. | Family Recollections based on emails | 35, 36 |
| XIX. | Resources | 37 |

# Belgian Family Tree:

Belgian "Godenne" Ancestry

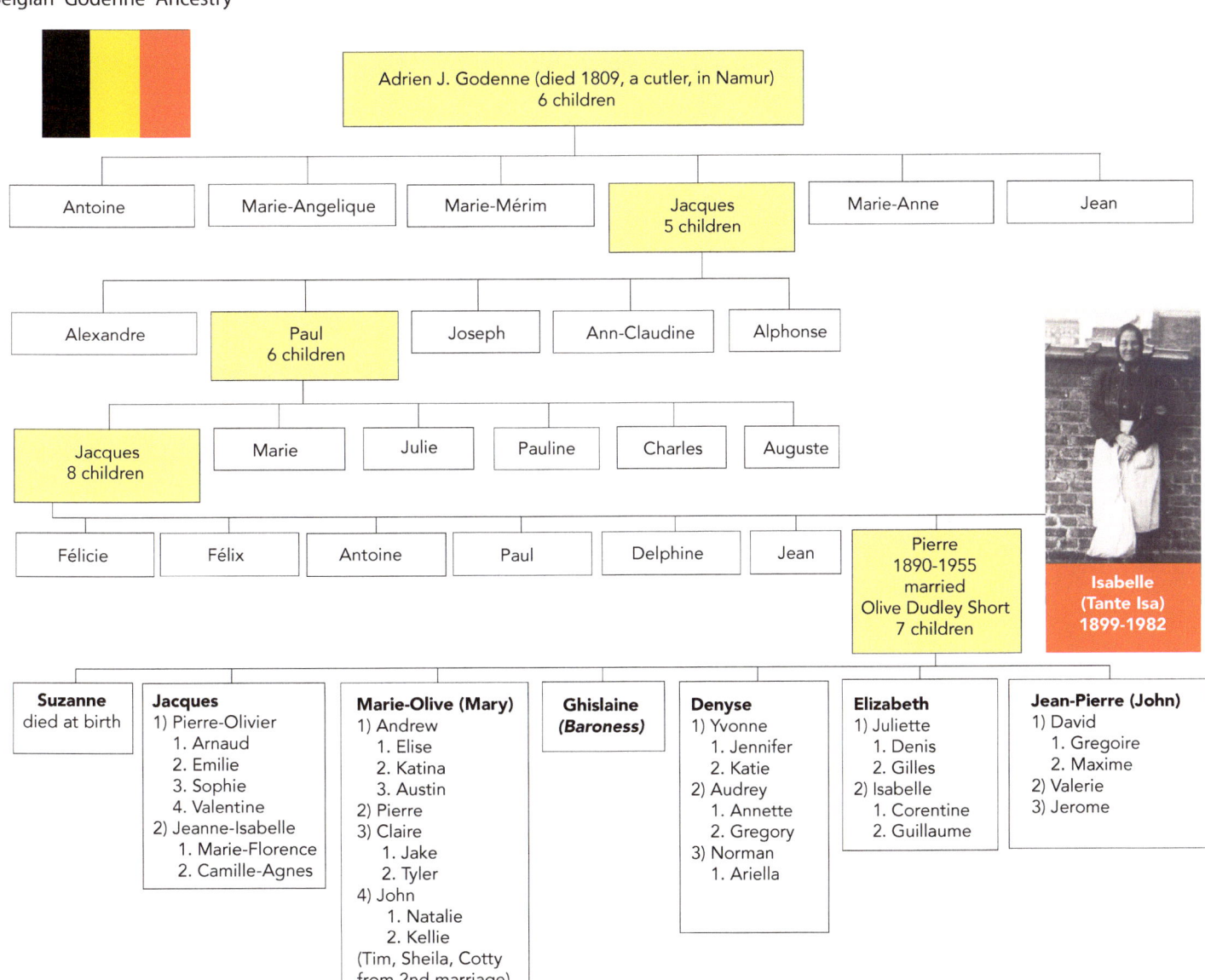

# British Family Tree:

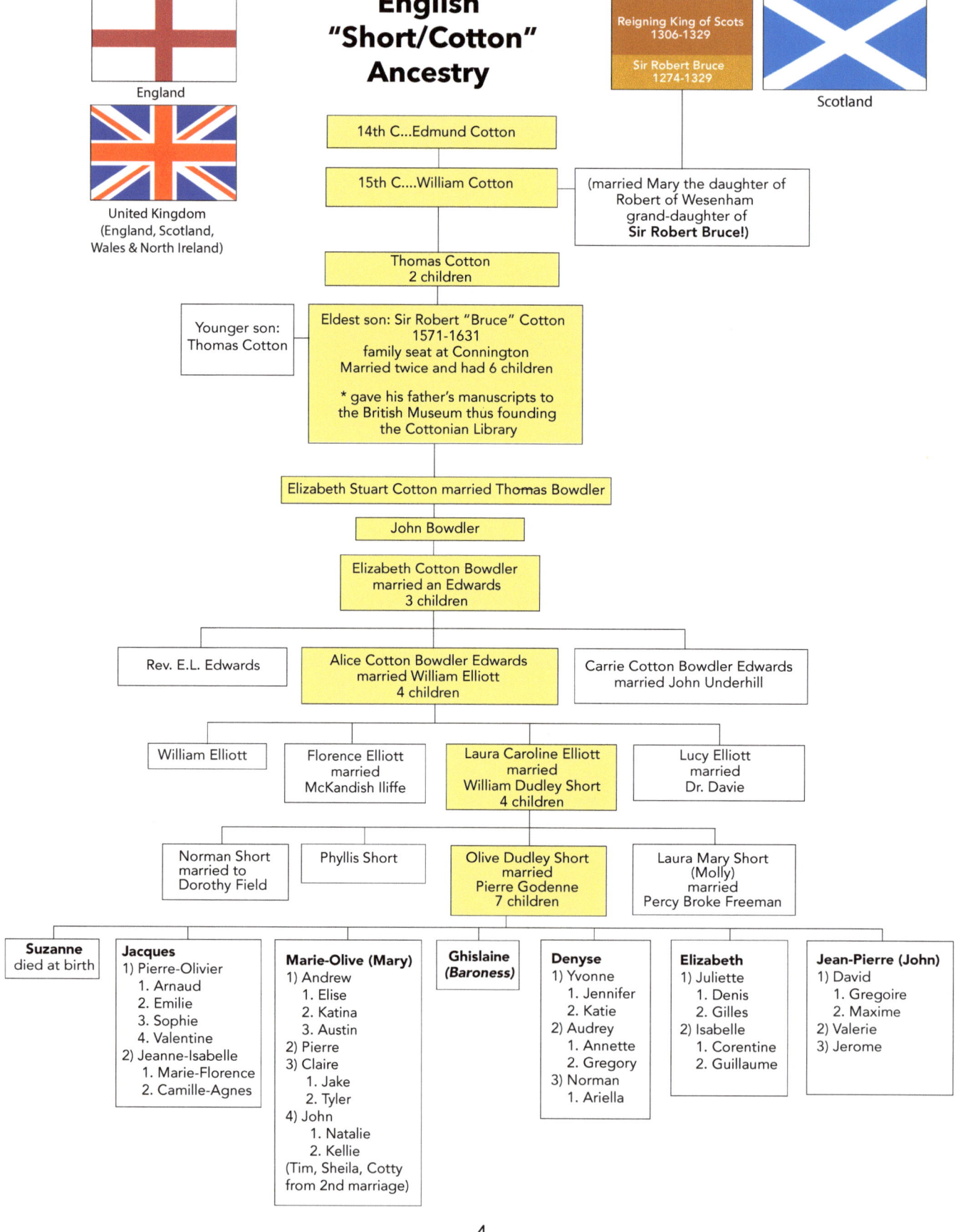

# "How Isabelle Godenne is connected to me and my cousins"

left to right; Isabelle Godenne, Mother's nurse, Pierre, her brother, Isa's & Pierre's mother Victoire, a local vicor

*Circa 1940 in Namur, Belgium*

**End of WWII and the German occupation of Belgium, Dr. Pierre Godenne's Family: left to right; Denyse, Mary, Jacques, Jean, Pierre - Dad/Papa (Belgian), Olive - Mom/Mum (British), Ghislaine, Elizabeth**
*Circa 1945 in Brussels, Belgium*

# Mlle Isabelle Godenne is "Tante Isa":

March 11, 1899 – August 12, 1982

*a member of the Belgian Resistance
whose secret military ID is shown below*

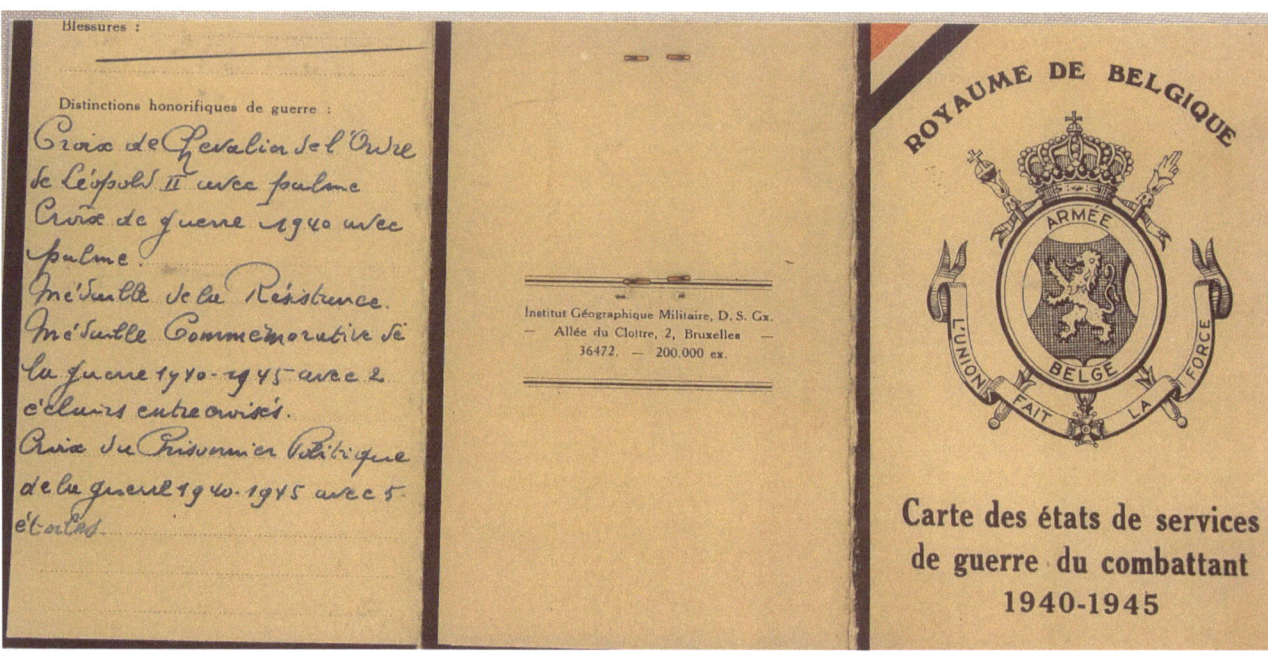

*"The only thing necessary for the triumph of evil is for good men to do nothing."*
- Edmund Burke, Irish Statesman

## ACKNOWLEDGEMENTS

My sincere appreciation goes to the Godenne extended family for sharing their information and/or memories of Tante Isa (our Great Aunt Isabelle Godenne). This material, combined with my own memories and research, helped me chronicle Tante Isa's story. I had always wanted to find out more and document Tante Isa's heroic role in the Belgian Resistance and her fate. The support and encouragement of my husband, and our two adult daughters reinforced my commitment to carry this through.

Although I am unsure who translated Tante Isa's file from German to French, I was informed that her niece, Elizabeth Godenne/Renard, did the work of typing it. The file reveals Tante Isa's trial, her sentencing, and other related events. In 2020 her daughters, Isabelle and Juliette, helped significantly by providing me the material which was key to the content and accuracy of Tante Isa's story. Furthermore, I was able to confirm and expand this information by acquiring the complete files from the Belgian War Archives. In addition, my cousin Isabelle Burki, was extremely helpful by sending me materials her father, Jacques Godenne, had saved regarding Tante Isa's importance in the Resistance. In so many ways, this was a group project.

Aside from the sources of this document, I want to credit our friend and graphic designer, Carole Drong, who did a remarkable job with the ancestry charts and all the photography used in this project. Your work, Carole, is truly appreciated.

It is also essential that I express thanks to my cousins who shared not just their memories and information, but their enthusiastic interest, as well as artifacts that had been entrusted to them. I am thankful that they wanted to share them with me for this project.

The greatest thanks, of course, goes to Tante Isa, herself, who chose to act in the face of evil. She was recruited by her local Vicar, Father George, to join in the fight against Nazi rule by serving as an interpreter for downed Allied pilots who only spoke English, but who needed help escaping occupied territory and returning to the United Kingdom. There is also some indication that she may have helped in other clandestine ways that will be mentioned later in this document.

I thank all of you!
Affectueusement,

*Yvonne Sims*

# PROLOGUE

I was born in 1949 and I am the oldest of all the cousins on my mother's side, the Godenne side, from Belgium. I was inspired to tell Tante Isa's story after reading a book called: **A Train In Winter** which is based on the memoires of imprisoned French Resistance women, as well as stories shared by their descendants. Always fascinated by the little bit I knew of Tante Isa, I realized that telling her story was a now or never moment. So, while isolating during the Covid-19 pandemic, I found the time I needed. My greatest fear has always been that her story would be lost. I used to tell it to my French students, and regretted that I couldn't answer their questions, like where was she imprisoned. Therefore, I promised myself to someday find out all I could, and then share her story with our family and beyond.

# MY RECOLLECTIONS OF TANTE ISA
## through my mother's point of view

For my mom, living in Belgium as a teenager during WWII meant living through the misery and desperation of German occupation and coping with the tragedies of war. The German occupation of Belgium lasted five long years: 1940 – 1945. During this time period, she would have been 14 – 19 years old. My brother, sister and I have heard many sad and horrific stories about this challenging time in her life. It made us aware there is much more to our Belgian heritage than its fine lace and delicious chocolates.

It would be fair to say that our mother, Denyse Godenne, was traumatized by the war (as I'm sure her siblings were, as well). Her happy, safe, comfortable world had been turned up-side-down. Growing up, we three children were struck by the fact she could never watch war shows or any kind of battles or violence on the screen. Once I remember her explaining to me that she didn't cry much after the war because she had no more tears left. It was a very sobering statement, and I realized her experiences must have haunted her.

One of her stories begins with her as a young girl in occupied Belgium, she was waiting for the trolley with her girl-friend to go to school. They heard air raid sirens and tried to take cover. Sadly, there was no time, so they only managed to huddle with each other on the ground. Her friend was hit by shrapnel and never got back up. Seeing death for the first time and losing a close friend must have been devastating. How does one fall asleep at night with the memories of such events. With the bombings, blood, and rubble, day to day life was frightening. Tensions ran high. Germans were on the streets everywhere amplifying the fear. Again, when she was a bit older, my mom's boyfriend whom she hoped to marry someday, was also killed. Life was a nightmare.

She explained about the scarcity of food and about ration cards, their value being continually reduced. There was no sugar or flour, or milk, or butter, or coffee. She said that to bake what resembled a cake, they had to crush up chestnuts to substitute for flour, and it tasted horrible. With food scarce, hunger became normal. Years later when I grew up, I didn't realize that it was unique that our Belgian mother insisted on putting in our basement, a huge pantry stocked with tons of canned goods that she called our "World War III supplies". What we thought was funny and even teased her about, was prompted by a very real dark memory.

Often she told us the celebrated Belgian story of the "Manneken Pis" (Dutch). In Brussels, I have seen the famous bronze fountain sculpture of a naked boy peeing. My mother believed the statue represented a brave little boy who defiantly faced the Germans in this manner. However, I now know her version is legend, not history. Yet, this legend attests to how rebellious many of the people of Belgium felt living under German oppression. I can still hear her using the angry French expression "Les Sales Boches!" (slang for Dirty Krauts!) when referring to the Germans with hatred and disgust.

[Manneken Pis which is Dutch for "Little Pissing Man is a 1618 landmark in the center of Brussels, Belgium (a country where half speak French and half Flemish). Today this statue is a symbol of defiance with many stories. The current statue is a replica dating from 1965.

One story is that the boy saved the city from a fire, another has him as the victim of a witche's spell for peeing on her door, or back in the 15th century it was used to distribute drinking water! The little boy is a legend and an icon for the city. It has become a great tourist attraction with many miniatures sold in various costumes.]

My mom was proud of her father, Pierre Godenne, and told us he had anticipated Hitler's brutal takeover, and therefore had converted much of the family money into gold to be able to provide for them by buying on the black market. I also remember her explaining how her father tried to have his family escape early-on by car through France into Spain. But they were stopped at the border of Spain and forced to return to Belgium. As a medical doctor with his own clinic, her father was disheartened that his clinic was taken over by the Germans and (if I remember correctly) he was forced to continue practicing there, helping German patients.

The most impressive story of all, was about her father's sister, Isabelle Godenne, Tante Isa (an affectionate term meaning Aunt Isa). In 1943, Tante Isa was a single woman in her early forty's.

She was one of eight Godenne children born in Belgium. Isabelle lived and worked in the family print/stationary shop in Namur, Belgium. The shop on Main street in the small town of Namur, had a fairly large apartment, even with a courtyard, in the back where she (and I believe her mother and perhaps a brother, Jean) lived. One of her brothers, Pierre (who she seemed especially close to) lived with his English wife, Olivia, and their six children (Jacques, Mary, Ghilly, Denyse, Jean, Elizabeth) in Brussels, Belgium, the capital. Pierre was a successful doctor with his own clinic. I don't know where in Belgium the other six siblings of Isabelle and Pierre lived during the German occupation, nor if they all survived the war. I can say that Pierre and his wife and six children did survive those harrowing years.

My mother made sure we children all got the chance to meet Isabelle Godenne, Tante Isa, our great aunt. We were actually able to visit her in her home in Namur, Belgium. I will refer to her simply as Tante Isa, throughout this recounting of her story of valor.

I believe most of my cousins also had the opportunity to meet her, and I have included their input concerning Tante Isa. Besides being a very devout Catholic, our Tante Isa was a wonderful, kind, generous and happy person. What I was astounded to learn was that in all my talks with either my mom, or Tante Isa herself, I was never once told (nor, as far as I know, anyone else) about the five medals of honor Tante Isa was awarded for her courageous work in the Belgian Resistance during WWII. Her description should include the words brave and humble, to be sure.

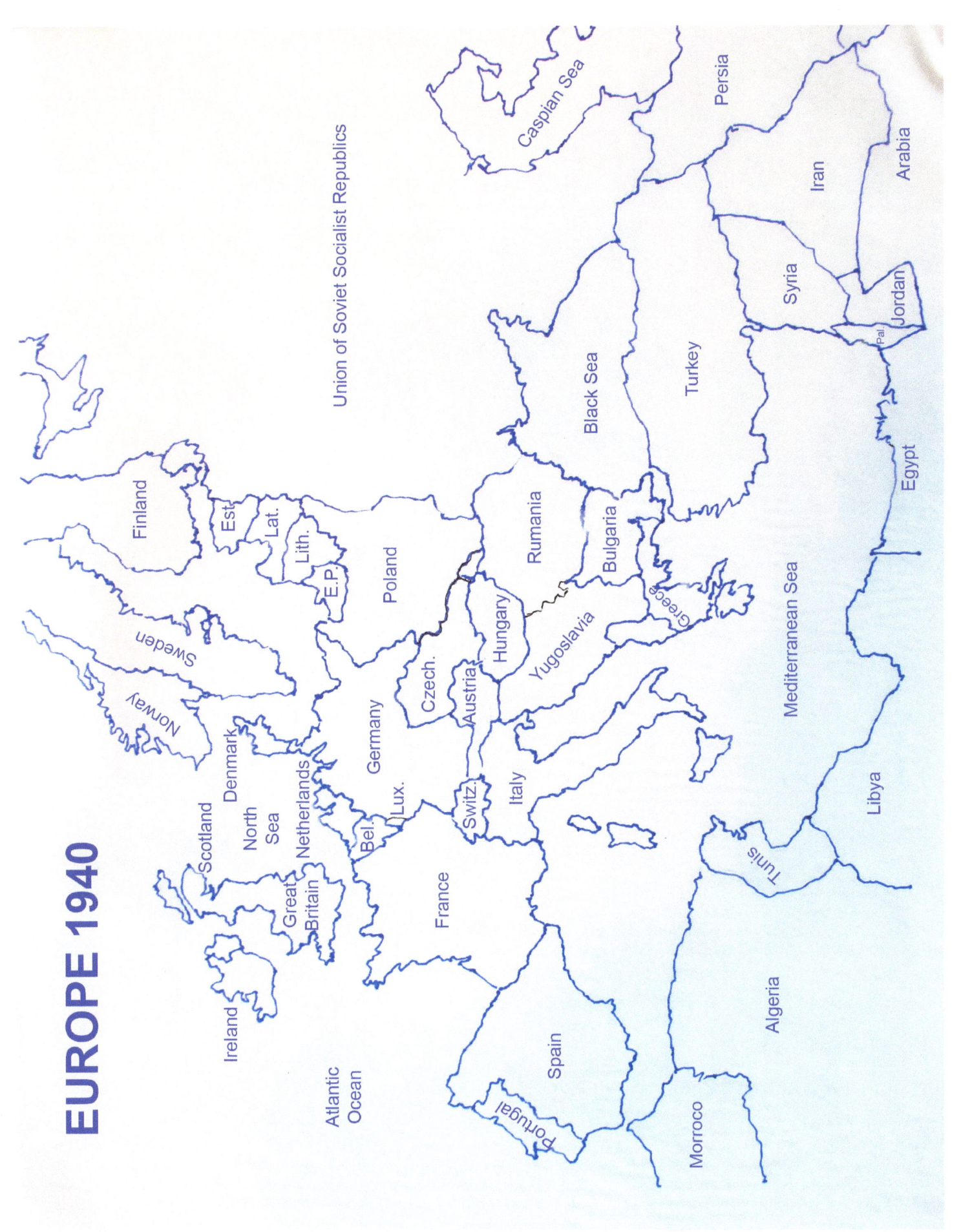

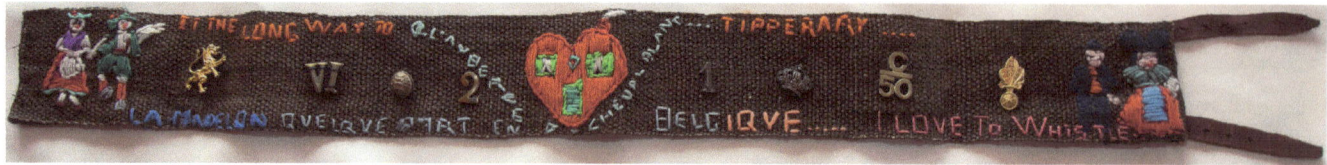

*(Tante Isa right after release, upper left; Her album title page with names of cities where prisoners were dropped off, upper right; her brother Jean + Isa 1965, middle; Godenne/Skaggs children with their Great Aunt Isa, mid-right; Obit 1982, bottom left; prison/war artifacts: belts, mug, album, bottom right; Isabelle Godenne/ Tante Isa 1899-1982, bottom right; Handmade belt from Waldheim prison, bottom)*

# RESISTANCE GROUPS:
## "ZERO SERVICE" and/or "COMETE RESEAU"

**Quandary:**

*I need to explain that in the death announcement for Tante Isa (found at the end of this manuscript) it states that she was part of a Resistance group called Zero. However, the Belgian War Archives sent me a volume of documentation confirming her participation in the group called Comet, as well as letters of honorary distinction for her courage. Therefore, it is my opinion that either the person who wrote the death announcement made an error or, perhaps, Tante Isa could have played a role in both groups, especially since she took over the family print/stationery shop which would have been valuable to the Resistance. What matters is that she was brave and selfless, helping those she could.*

**Various Resistance Groups:**

During the German occupation of Belgium (1939-1945), the struggle for freedom and the need to resist quickly surfaced. The German government levied heavy taxes on the people of Belgium as well as other occupied countries. Food, clothing and fuel were scarce because almost everything was given to the German troops. Many civilians were taken and conscripted to work in German factories.

In the beginning, underground activity was carried out by individuals or small groups, despite the danger. Eventually there were at least 15 large organized Resistance groups, and as many as 25 other smaller groups formed hoping to help topple the German/Nazi rule. Intuitively, the many different networks of Resistance worked separately from each other for protection from the consequences of infiltration by German spies. In this way, to be caught would not mean the end of all the Resistance networks.

The names of some of these Belgian Resistance groups follow. The first four were well known for specializing in the escape of prisoners and downed pilots via an underground network of many different routes and contacts.

1. Zero Service
2. Luc (later to be called Marc)
3. Komeet Line
4. Comète Nationale de FL = Milices Patriotiques = MP
5. White Brigade from Antwerp
6. FL = Front de l"Independence
7. Solidarité
8. Armée Belge de Patriots or Partisan Armies
9. EVA = Evasion
10. Group G
11. Belgian Communist Party
12. Legion Belge = Armée Sécrete – the original Belgian military that went underground.
    Its headquarters were in London, England.

**Zero Service & Comet Line Roles**

Zero was a clandestine group that became a large Belgian underground network. It collected both economic and political information as well as military intelligence. With this information couriers were sent down through occupied France to the coasts of Spain and Portugal to get this valuable intel to Great Britain. Zero secretly published "La Libre Belgique" which was very difficult given the scarcity of paper, ink and access to printers, not to mention the challenge of distribution. I suspect that Tante Isa's stationery/print shop might have been involved in this endeavor, but I have no conclusive evidence of this.

Another service performed by both Resistance groups, Zero and Comet Line, was their secret escape routes or "underground railroads" (a term originally coined to refer to the secret escape routes for runaway slaves in the U.S.A., but which I will continue to use here in quotes). The Resistance helped people on the run, like escaped prisoners of war fleeing the Germans, or downed Allied pilots, who needed to get back to Great Britain so they could continue their service. Usually the goal was to reach the British Consulate in Bilbao, Spain. Unfortunately, the Germans tried to infiltrate these patriotic groups and sometimes succeeded.

Nevertheless, in three years the Comet Line was able to help 776 airmen. Their network consisted of about 3,000 civilians of which 700 were arrested and 290 executed or died in prison.

What follows is Tante Isa's impressive role (punishable by death or imprisonment) which did not involve weapons or violence, but rather the simple effort of helping those in danger trying to escape. It is well known that posters were put up by the Nazis warning civilians not to help downed airmen. Furthermore, there were hefty rewards offered to report anyone aiding airmen. Nazis did not want downed pilots returning to Great Britain where they would be able to re-deploy and bomb German troops, arms depots, and other assets. The Resistance underground networks operated against high stakes.

# TRANSLATIONS

## *FROM FRENCH TO ENGLISH*

A. I have taken the liberty to summarize how Tante Isa's Resistance participation evolved, then the path of her detentions, and a record of her correspondence with her brothers based on the notes given to me by my cousin Juliette Renard.

B. With some commentary of my own, I have given a fairly rigid translation of the transcripts of Tante Isa's trial and sentencing, based on records sent to me by my cousin Isabelle Renard and then further supported and expanded by the transcripts received from the Belgian War Archives "Cega Soma".

Items included in this section are:

#1.  Isabelle Godenne's background introduced at her trial, April 17, 1943
      by the Luftwaffe Tribunal
#2.  Summary of her crime against the German Reich
#3.  Description of the situation with presumed Allied Pilot #1
#4.  Description of the situation with presumed Allied Pilot #2
#5.  Luftwaffe Tribunal accusation, Tante Isa's defense
#6.  The verdicts and sentencing
#7.  Her internments and transfers with extra details about prison facilities,
      and her final destination of Waldheim Prison, Germany

# A. Overview of Tante Isa's participation in the Resistance, her arrest, and the path of her detentions, as well as, her correspondence with her brothers.

Isabelle Godenne (Tante Isa) was 44 years old, a single woman living in Namur, Belgium. Here, she owned and managed the family's printing and stationery shop during the German occupation of WWII (Sept.1, 1939 - Sept. 2,1945). She was recruited by the local Vicar: Father George and became an active member of the "Comete Reseau" (Comet Network) and perhaps the "Service Zero" also. Both were secret Belgian Resistance groups. As far as I could learn, only her obituary confirms her membership in the group called Service Zero, whereas there is much documentation of her participation in Comet.

Knowing English fairly well, she served as a translator, and played a significant part in the "underground railroad" helping people who needed to flee. They needed shelter, food, and a translator to survive. Unfortunately, after who knows how many successful missions, she was deceived by one of the individuals she tried to help. She and her partners thought they were dealing with a downed Allied pilot who later turned out to be a disguised Nazi. She and her friends/associates were all arrested as political prisoners against the Reich and put on trial: April 17, 1943. The details of this trial are shown in the following pages.

Her first detention was in the Prison of St. Gilles, cell # 387, in Brussels, Belgium. This Belgian prison was controlled by the Germans. All the rules in this prison were in German and had to be translated into French if the prisoners were to understand, let alone obey. Needless to say, this made a terrifying situation even more difficult.

Fortunately, someone in our family kept a record of correspondence from Isabelle (Tante Isa) and the attempts of her brothers, especially Pierre and Paul (see "ancestry charts") to help her. The first letter from her came April 29,1943. Then on May 11, 1943 there was a letter from her brother Pierre Godenne (my/our grandfather) to their brother Paul Godenne reporting on Pierre's visit and organizing future visits, as well as care packages for their sister, Isabelle. They might also have taken her dirty laundry with its secret notes hidden in tiny bits in the knitting of her handmade socks. There were another two letters from Tante Isa (Isabelle): May 13, and May 27, 1943. Unfortunately, over the later years, no one seems to have kept track of the letters written during her captivity.

On Sept. 6, 1943, her brothers tried a new strategy. Pierre again wrote to Paul about drafting a letter in German requesting that Isabelle be released on parole (on appeal). This letter was sent Sept. 12, 1943 addressed to General von Falkenhausen. Acknowledgement of its receipt came Sept. 18, 1943 with a resulting negative reply on Sept. 24,1943. Despite their disappointment, her brothers refused to give up.

Her oldest nephew and niece, Jacques and Mary, (children of Pierre, my/our grandfather) visited her (as I understand it), but it was "counter-productive" (the exact significance of this wording is unclear). Soon thereafter, Isabelle was moved to the Forest Prison, also in Brussels, near the St. Gilles Prison. Isabelle was able to write two more letters: Oct. 20, 1943 and Nov. 1, 1943.

Her brother, Paul transmitted a group letter to her on Nov. 10, 1943. Unfortunately, on Nov. 11, 1943 there was a disturbing correspondence from Isabelle saying she was being deported out of the country to Waldheim Prison, Saxony, Germany! This meant her circumstances would go from bad to much worse.

However, her brothers doubled their efforts to get her freed. Pierre sent two letters on Nov.14,1943: one to the Ambassador of Repatriation with the Red Cross; and the other to Your Eminence the Cardinal – Monseigneur Micara (Apostolic Nuncio) requesting intervention by the Vatican. Pierre shared copies of these two last ditch efforts with his brothers Paul and Jean. However, to the family's dismay, their desperate attempts were to no avail. Tante Isa was sent to Germany.

At Waldheim Prison, Saxony, Germany the rules forbid prisoners to write for the first six months after which time, they were allowed to write and receive one letter every six weeks! The rigidity of this mandate must have severely impacted prisoner morale. For the younger generation reading this, please know that letter writing was the key to communication during this time period. There existed some phone landlines, but prisoners would have no access to such a convenience. Furthermore, there was no such thing as cell phones, nor computers.

Without letters, a prisoner would be completely cut off from family and friends, not to mention being in a foreign country where she did not know the language. The sense of isolation must have been devastating. There is a record of only four letters from Tante Isa while in Waldheim Prison: April 20, May 14, June 25, and Aug. 6, 1944. Yet, her liberation did not happen until almost a year later, May 7, 1945.

## B. With some commentary of my own, I have given a fairly rigid translation of the transcripts of Tante Isa's trial, defense, and sentencing.

*Items included in this section are:*

### #1. Isabelle Godenne's background introduced at her trial, April 17, 1943 by the Luftwaffe Tribunal

The accused, Isabelle Godenne, daughter of a printer, was born March 11, 1899. She attended primary school and then middle school until age 16 and then did two years of school beyond that. After her schooling and the death of her father, she took over the printing business in Namur which her mother had continued running. This print shop became in the following years an "anonymous society". (The meaning of this statement is unclear to me. But, it makes me wonder about its possible role in the Zero Service.) The accused continued to work there. She was never subjected to any "condemnations" (again this term is confusing) and yet she was arrested twice: Jan. 13-15, 1943 and again April 15,1943, but went before the German Court Tribunal, in Brussels April 17,1943.

Tante Isa was one of six Belgian friends from Namur arrested in connection with an "underground railroad" that the Germans infiltrated. They had no real proof, but enough evidence to demonstrate that these six individuals had helped two disguised Allied pilots whom they believed were enemies to the Germans. These resistance activists were accused of helping these pilots hide and then escape. Such serious charges met with severe consequences and often the death penalty. Prison sentences, even short ones, were equally horrific since many prisoners never survived their full term no matter how short.

### #2. Summary of the crime against the German Reich at her trial:

Two presumably downed Allied pilots were pointed in the direction of a Belgian named Bertrand by an anonymous local Belgian countryman. These pilots were seeking shelter and help finding a way out of Belgium via the "underground railroad". Being disguised as Allied pilots, these Nazis had been told that this "underground railroad" was somehow connected to a lawyer named Albert Melot who was suspected to be the leader of a Resistance group in Namur.

These pilots wanted Bertrand to take them to Melot's home, but he claimed to not know where that was. Melot himself moved around a lot trying to avoid capture. Therefore, Bertrand took them instead to the home of Father George, because in Namur it was well known that Father Georges was a good friend of Melot since they worked together with youth organizations. Father Georges welcomed these phony Allied pilots with open arms and when he got a chance he called Melot to alert him and ask what to do.

Melot came immediately and gave instructions to transfer the pilots after he questioned them. Melot was very suspicious of these pilots, but had nothing concrete to prove their story was false.

To begin with, Melot wanted the two pilots separated. One pilot was to sleep at Father Georges' house, but first they (Pilot #1 and Father Georges) went for dinner at the home of the Deroyer sisters.

Meanwhile, the other Pilot #2 was taken by Melot, to the Davreux family home first. However, the circumstances of this encounter are in a special report that I could not access. Next, they went to the Guignon family home. Here Pilot #2 ate generous meals (considering the sad state of rationed food), and spent two nights on his own with the Guignon family.

### #3. The Situation of the Presumed Allied Pilot #1:

At the Deroyer home, the sisters, Leonie and Jeanne, lived with their 84-year-old mother. The three ladies warmly welcomed Father Georges and the presumed Allied Pilot #1. They managed to offer the group a substantial meal despite the scarcity of food. According to the pre-trial transcripts, Father Georges denies ever introducing the pilot as British or American, although at trial the German pilot claimed he did. Nevertheless, the Luftwaffe Tribunal insisted that it was obvious to the Belgian sisters the purpose of their visit.

At first, the conversation with the downed pilot was very difficult because he claimed to only speak English. Therefore, Father Georges called his good friend, Isabelle Godenne, to come join them and be their translator. Isabelle/Tante Isa did not initially know the Deroyer sisters. Over the course of the evening, everyone relaxed and opened up. Unfortunately, Father Georges and the ladies expressed their opinion that all Germans should be eliminated. One of the Deroyer sisters even offered a special "Belgian Victory Pin" to the downed pilot. They explained he should accept it because according to the Allied plans they had heard, the war would end in three or four months with an American invasion.

The presumed Allied Pilot #1 told Isabelle (Tante Isa) he was with the Royal Airforce (RAF) and that he had been shot down over Namur, Belgium. He then explained to all of them, through Isabelle's translating skills, the story of his life and family. His entire story seemed to make sense to them. In the end, the downed Pilot #1 proclaimed that due to their kindness and generous support he would return to fight against Nazi Germany to help Belgium win its freedom.

The second night, Father Georges returned with Pilot # 1 to the Deroyer sisters' home to again have dinner with Isabelle Godenne as translator. Beforehand, per the pilot's request, Tante Isa gave him a white, civilian shirt so he could better blend in during his escape out of Belgium.

So, for two evenings the Pilot #1 ate at the Deroyer sisters' and then returned to sleep at Father Georges' home. The third day Father Georges woke his guest and presented him with his boots, newly resoled and polished as a gift. After lunch and packing up some food for the road, Melot arrived with the other Pilot #2. Finally, the two pilots and Melot traveled in secret to Brussels to begin their journey out of Belgium, or so Melot and the others thought.

### #4. The Situation of the Presumed Allied Pilot #2:

Meanwhile, that first evening, Melot took the Allied Pilot #2 first to the Davreux family, but this part of the story became the subject of a special German report not available in Tante Isa's file. I can only guess what might have happened to the Davreux family.

Later that same evening around 8:00 pm Melot guided Pilot #2 to the home of retired Captain Maurice Guignon and his wife, Desirée Guignon, and their 21-year-old daughter. The Pilot #2 stayed for two nights enjoying generous dinners considering the scarcity of food. Their dinner conversation was helped along via an English-French dictionary.

Unfortunately, this unsuspecting family also managed to express their hatred of the Germans. They even praised the Allied bombing of the Ruhr valley where a Nazi industrial base was located and much of Hitler's munitions were manufactured. Furthermore, Captain Guignon bragged that his radio had a special frequency or device to allow him to listen to the English broadcasts when they were given in French. On top of that fact, Captain Guignon shared the fact that he and his family had previously sheltered a Russian escaped prisoner, also a pilot who had been shot down. He proudly spoke of helping him evade the Germans.

## #5. Luftwaffe Tribunal's ACCUSATION against Tante Isa:
### (the trial took place in German occupied Brussels, Belgium)

It has been proven without a doubt that Isabelle Godenne gave a white, civilian shirt to the Allied Pilot #1. She is accused of collaborating with others to harbor and feed the enemy (the disguised Pilot #1), furnishing direct aid to the enemy during the war against Germany. Helping a downed enemy pilot to return to his forces and with intent to destroy Nazi Germany is a serious crime.

### Tante Isa's Defense statement:

"I, Isabelle Godenne, was summoned to the Deroyer sisters' home by Father Georges without knowing what exactly it was about. He simply said he needed me to translate. She explained she only served as translator, for the pleasure of refreshing her English-speaking skills. Lastly, Isabelle, claimed that the "white shirt" was given simply as a result of her good-hearted nature. She had one at home, so she brought what he asked for, nothing more."

(It seems that Tante Isa must have somehow kept her calm. Her clever wit and innocent demeanor also evidently helped when sentencing was handed out. There is no indication from her German file that she ever divulged anything about the Comet Network or the Zero Service, nor her active part in any underground escape routes.)

## #6. The Verdicts: all were found guilty!!! – Sentencing:

1. Father Georges.................8 years in prison
2. Deroyer sister....................4 years in prison
3. Deroyer sister....................4 years in prison
4. Isabelle Godenne...............2.5 years in prison
5. Captain Guignon................death
6. Desirée Guignon................15 years in prison

## END OF TRAIL TRANSCRIPT TRANSLATIONS

Sadly, everyone arrested in this group died during the first two years of their sentence, except Tante Isa. Frustratingly, I could find no information on whether Bertrand, or Attorney Albert Melot, were ever caught.

However, I did discover in the files from the Belgian War Archives that Melot was the head of the Comet Line in Namur and that he signed a Letter of Honorary Distinction for Isabelle Godenne regarding her brave work in the Resistance. Albert Melot recommended the "Croix de Chevalier de L'Ordre de Leopold II" on July 30,1945. So, Melot must have lived to complete her file. This file also showed a letter of appreciation signed by US Army Chief Marshall on February 27, 1947.

*Saint Gilles Prison in Brussels, Belgium*

## #7. Prison and Transfers with extra details about the prison facilities

Tante Isa was first taken to **Saint Gilles**, a local prison controlled by the German military during the occupation. It is still the main prison in Brussels, and very overcrowded even today. This medieval type prison has five wings, that radiate from the central hub, and it is three stories high. Prisoners live in small cells resembling bare stone caves. It is said to have the smell of cabbage and urine. The plaque at the main entrance reads:

« N'oublions jamais!!! Trent mille patriotes, résistants, hommes, femmes, enfants, connurent ici les prémieres heures de leur long martyre, du 17 Mai 1940 au 3 Septembre 1944. Jamais les menaces et les supplices n'eurent raison, ni de leur courage ni de leur foi. »

"Never forget!!! Thirty thousand patriots, members of the resistance, men, women, children, all knew here the first hours of their long martyrdom from the 17th May 1940 to the 3rd September 1944. Threats and torture never got the better of their courage nor their faith."

At some point, Tante Isa was transferred from St. Gilles to the nearby Forest Prison also in Brussels. It was built in 1910 like a fortress for 360 prisoners, but is also still used today and is overcrowded. It has four wings – two where 3 prisoners were held in cells meant for one (they would eat there and share a toilet). The other 2 wings, the prisoners had individual cells with no running water – they used a bucket that could go unemptied for 48 hours or more (this situation hopefully has changed today).

To her dismay, Tante Isa was eventually deported to Waldheim Prison in Saxony, Germany. I have been in touch with the current archivist at Waldheim Prison, Doreen Wustig, who sent me a copy of the old "access book" page showing Tante Isa's entry date as Dec. 21, 1943.

Isabelle Godenne's entry number was 460, while her prisoner number was 8026 (which was not tattooed on her person according to Doreen Wustig). Following is an article I found on the internet that explains what her experience at Waldheim must have been like, as it was written by another female prisoner there.

# "The Women in Waldheim Prison" by Gabriele Hackl

*Based on information gathered from novels by Eva Lippold.*
*Eva Lippold was a Resistance fighter who spent 5 years at Waldheim Prison.*

Waldheim Prison was the largest and most important women's prison in the German Reich. It served both men and women, but in separate facilities. In 1926 the women's institution fell under the direction of Dr. Else Voigtlander. She was a renowned psychologist serving as director through 1945. Tante Isa was sent there in 1943. Dr. Voigtlander is described by Eva Lippold in her novel: **Living Where There is Death,** as very masculine in voice and appearance, someone who even smoked cigars.

There was both physical and psychological mistreatment of prisoners during the Nazi era. The increase in deaths reflected insufficient food, inadiquate medical care and ever-increasing work. The women prisoners differed greatly from each other in terms of: the reason they were there, the length of stay, their age, nationality, religion, profession, etc. Many were convicted of theft, fraud, war economy crimes like counterfeit ration cards, illegal slaughtering, illicit trading; few were murderers. Resistance fighters were considered political prisoners.

Political prisoners, like Tante Isa, experienced special hardships as they were denied promotions in the hierarchical prison system which later became the Nazi era system of performance rewards. They would never be allowed to work as domestic help because it allowed more freedom of movement and contact with others. However, the political prisoners did not regard their crimes as immoral acts. Understandably, they felt morally superior. Still they established friendly relationships with the criminal prisoners.

In the book **A Train In Winter**, by Caroline Moorehead, it was emphasized that women apparently stood a better chance of survival than men because of their tendency to look out for one another and bond. Men tend to show strength by being independent. Moorehead explained that the friendships women developed promoted morale during their captivity which helped with their survival.

Administrators at Waldheim Prison frequently made biased decisions favoring their fellow countrymen. During the shortages of war time, the German prisoners were provided for first, while the foreigners like Tante Isa received the worst clothes, and many suffered with no coats, bedding, or socks. To be precise, clothing items for non-Germans were either too small or too large, damaged, or meager protection against the cold or wet weather. Clothing in general was scarce, as well as personal hygiene products.

There was major overcrowding in Waldheim Prison especially of female prisoners. From 1939-1944 the number of female prisoners was quintupled while the number of males only doubled. The Waldheim Women's Prison had a maximum capacity of about 450 people, yet in July 1943 it had passed the 1,000 mark, which is when Tante Isa arrived.

Hackl (author of "The Women in Waldheim Prison") points out through the stories told by Eva Lippold, that the most urgent concerns of the imprisoned women were medical care and the scarcity of food. However, the treatment of prisoners by female staff worsened over time becoming increasingly brutal and callous.

Work was expected by all prisoners. Traditional types of jobs for female prisoners were crafts such as knitting, embroidery, sewing, making nets, or rolling cigars. They were providing nurses uniforms, socks, and cigars for the German army. Some were put to work as domestic workers in the prisons. Many were sent to private companies as forced laborers for wartime production manufacturing parts for cars, tanks, machine guns, and planes as well as doing transport and agricultural work. If companies could not set up shop within the prison walls, prisoners were moved to satellite prison work camps. I did not discover what kind of work was forced on Tante Isa. However, I wonder if it involved some kind of weaving since she made the woven belt she gave me and I have saved with other memorabilia from her prison experience.

Living together in extremely confined space due to the severe overcrowding was both a physical and psychological challenge. Oddly, even harmless friendly intimacy was discouraged and could incur severe punishment. However, prisoners sometimes entered into opportunistic relationships with free workers at the site of outside companies where they worked. Sexual favors might be exchanged for food or for simply smuggling out letters.

In Oct. 1944 the German prison facilities near the front were abandoned. Then in Feb. 1945 institutions further inland in the Old Reich were vacated and the prisoners moved even further inland. These prisoners had to travel in part by foot, occasionally also by train without being equipped for winter. Many did not survive these marches. Thousands of men prisoners, who were classified as dangerous, were left behind and murdered by firing squads. Gratefully, Tante Isa was not subjected to either of these fates.

## Tante Isa's Liberation

At the end of the war, there were some Nazi prisons that made a peaceful transfer to the Allied forces. At other institutions, the officials and administrators simply took off, leaving the prisoners to await their liberation by Allied forces.

Documentation shows that the Russian Red Army liberated the Waldheim Women's Prison on May 7, 1945. Exactly how this transpired, or how violent, I never learned. I do know that the central office of the prison was "pillaged" (the exact term used in the records.) Fortunately, Tante Isa was evidently strong enough and determined enough to get hold of her personal file from that office. But whether there was a battle or the prison guards all fled before the Russians arrived, I do not know. The important thing is that our Tante Isa lived to be freed after serving two horrible years of her sentence.

## As a side note:

I would like to mention that many years later during the summer of 1965, my sister (13) and I (16) spent two weeks living with Tante Isa. We lived in the rear apartment behind the connected print/stationery shop. Occasionally, she spoke to us a bit about those terrible years in a Nazi prison. I recall her explaining that of all her group who were arrested, she was the sole survivor. My cousin Claire also remembers being told this. It must have been a hard truth for Tante Isa to accept. There was also the haunting fact that she didn't know the welfare of her brothers or their families back home while she was imprisoned and on her passage by military convoy home.

As previously stated, Tante Isa credited her faith for her survival. She asserts her Catholic faith on the outside first page of her file. Her own easily recognizable long hand, introduces her prison file as a cover page. She also explained having been blessed with extra weight going into her ordeal. So many prisoners simply starved to death. She herself dropped to a mere 80 pounds. The woven belt she made for herself (that she gave to me) is not quite 28" long, indeed, a pretty narrow waist.

I remember asking her if her missing eye was a result of the prison experience, but she said no. I learned later that she had a childhood disease that required the removal of her eye. She did however share that during her captivity, she had witnessed terrible mistreatment and torture. She told a story of a women prisoner who had done something wrong according to her captors. As punishment, they taped her hands closed in a fist so that not only could she not use her fingers, but over time her fingernails would grow painfully through the fleshy part of her hands. This was pure torture. There was also a notation in Tante Isa's album mentioning that their hair had been shaved off. We can only imagine what else they all endured.

Overall, my conversations with Tante Isa about the war and her imprisonment, revealed a strong woman who showed no indication of feeling sorry for herself, nor was she bitter. She did what she believed was right. She really was amazing. She lived to be 83 years old, dying of natural causes in her beloved hometown of Namur in 1982. Her funeral mass and burial announcement are included at the end of this manuscript.

*US Army trucks with liberated prisoners returning to their homes*

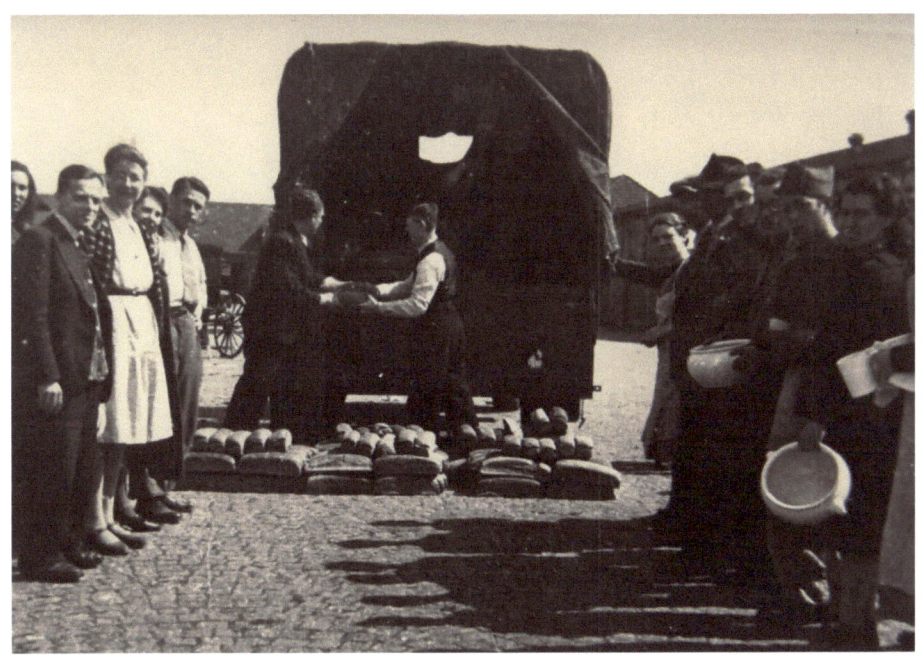
*Russian truck giving out soup and bread*

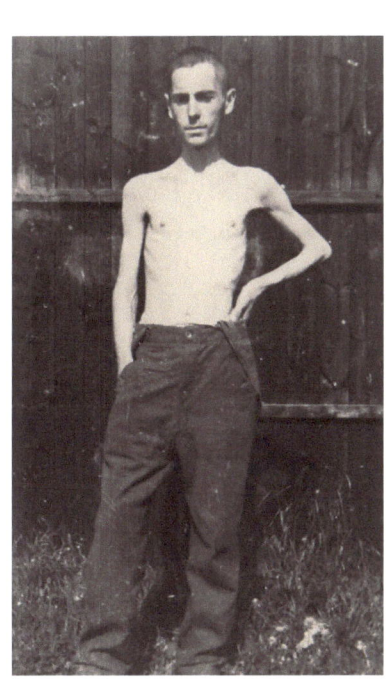
*One of fellow prisoners Le Pouilleux–a flea and lice ridden person May 1945*

# Forever a Devout Catholic

After Tante Isa's liberation and return home, at some point she wrote this powerful statement as a testament to her faith during her ordeal and beyond.

CECI EST MON TESTAMENT...
AU NOM DU PERE, DU FILS ET DU SAINT-ESPRIT !
QUE DIEU VOUS DONNE LA PAIX ! J'AI BIEN GARDE MA FOI. JE
REMERCIE LE SEIGNEUR DE ME L'AVOIR DONNEE. J'Y ADHERE DE
TOUTES LES FORCES DONT JE DISPOSE, DE MON CŒUR ET DE MON
ESPRIT. JE LE REMERCIE DE M'AVOIR DONNE UNE SAINTE MAMAN.
APRES MOI, PLUS PERSONNE NE SAURA CE QU'ELLE A ETE, UNE
SAINTE AUTHENTIQUE, J'ADORE ET J'AIME LA SAINTE TRINITE,
PERE, FILS ET ESPRIT. LA MESSE A ETE POUR MOI UN TRESOR.
J'AIME ET JE VENERE LA VIERGE PARIE. J'AIME L'EGLISE, JE
N'AI D'INIMITIE POUR PERSONNE.
JE VOUDRAIS QUE TOUS SOIENT HEUREUX

**The translation follows:**

## THIS IS MY TESTAMENT...

In the name of the Father, the Son and the Holy Spirit!
May God give you peace! I have kept my faith. I
thank the Lord to have given it to me. I adhere to it with
all the strength that I possess, with my heart and my
soul. I thank Him for having given me the Holy Mother.
In my opinion, no one will know that she was an
authentic saint. I adore and I love the Holy Trinity,
Father, Son, and Holy Spirit. The Mass was for me a treasure.
I love and I venerate the Virgin Mary. I love the Church.
I have hatred for no one. I would like everyone to be happy...

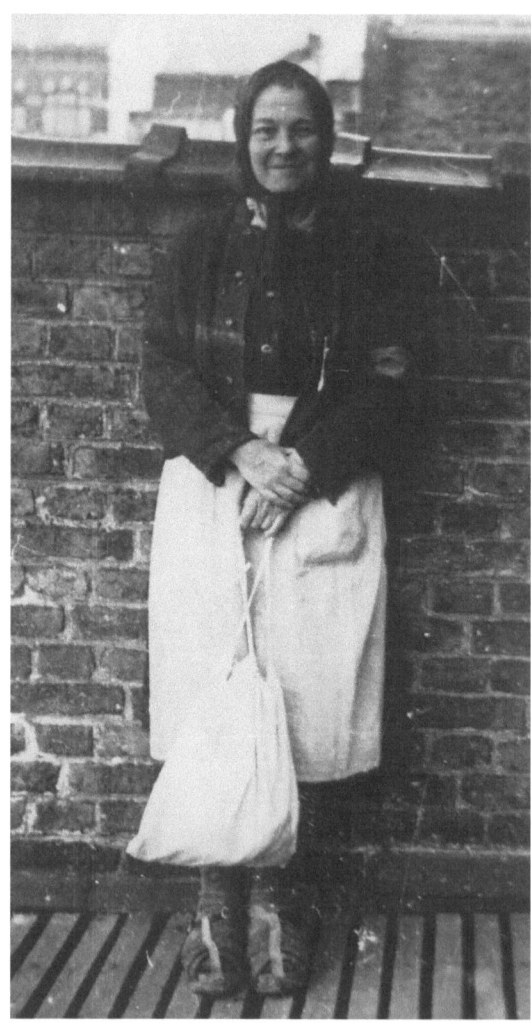

# ARTIFACTS and MEMORIBILIA

#1. Tante Isa gave me a **rough, woven, almost burlap-type belt** that she had made during her internment. This belt is about 2.75 inches wide and 28 inches long. It is decorated with odds and ends that she found. There are buttons, pins, numbers, a standing lion, and a crown. All these items are in metal. But, quite remarkable is the colorful embroidery that seems to reflect her spirit and her ability to find joy in the simple things in life. Some of the letters are hard to make out, so the spelling may be off.

Here is a description of the artwork and the quotes on her belt.

There are two embroidered couples designed at each end of the belt.

In the middle - a large, red heart with door, windows on each side, a chimney with smoke:

On each side of this red, heart house are words: A L'AUBERGE ...de CHEVAL ALANT
( At the inn...of the {going ?} horse)

Along the top of the belt is the quote: IT {is} THE LONG WAY TO TIPPERARY...

Along the bottom of the belt is: LA MADELON QUELQUE PART EN BELGIQUE
    (The Madeleine {a specially shaped soft cookie} somewhere in Belgium)

Also, along the bottom is the joyous statement: **I LOVE TO WHISTLE**

These embroidered words make one wonder what meaning may lie behind them. I would love to discuss with my cousins their thoughts about this idea someday. Given the circumstances of looming death and being surrounded by misery, it seems very probable that her word choices have deep significance beyond the surface meaning.

#2. Aunt Ghilly (Ghislaine Godenne) gave me a **Nazi soldier's belt**. She had saved it as a souvenir of the German occupation of Belgium that she and her 5 siblings endured.

#3. Tante Isa kept the **heavy, tin mug** she used in the Waldheim prison. She passed it on to her niece, Mary Godenne, who then passed it on to her children. John McCrea, her youngest child and my cousin, ended up with it and decided to add it to my collection of memorabilia supporting Tante Isa's story. I understand that there was also a metal plate, but that has been lost over the years.

#4. John McCrea (son of Mary Godenne), also made a wonderful find when he accidently discovered a **small album created by Tante Isa** after the war. It is a small elegant looking, tan album 8" x 10". It lists all the towns her liberation convoy passed through while returning prisoners to their homes. It documents her 16-day journey back to Namur, Belgium. She calls the album: "Retour de Captivité". It even has photos of Tante Isa in her many layered outfit of tattered clothing and head scarf. She had told me how very thin she had become but the clothing hides that fact until you compare it to photos of her before the ordeal. More detail about this album will follow.

The clothes Tante Isa wore in prison were eventually cleaned and donated to the Center of Studies and Documentation of the Auschwitz Foundation by my Aunt Elizabeth. Another interesting fact is that Tante Isa made a replica doll of herself in the identical outfit of her return from Nazi prison. She showed it to me and my sister when we visited her in 1965. Unfortunately, this item has been lost but it matched the photo of her in the album.

#5. Isabelle Burki (daughter of Jacques Godenne) sent me a photo album belonging to her father showing that time period. It contains precious family photos especially ones of Tante Isa before she was taken.

#6. Isabelle Burki also sent me a copy of Tante Isa's **military service record:**

«Carte des états de services de guerre du combattant 1940-1945 »
It has a clear photo of Tante Isa as a young woman and gives her rank and assignment.

#7. This military ID card also lists the **five medals of honorary distinction** awarded to Tante Isa for bravery in the Resistance during WWII. You can find them pictured on the internet, they are impressive and quite beautiful.

They are:
1. Croix de Chevalier de l'Ordre de Leopold II avec palme
2. Croix de Guerre 1940 avec palme
3. Médaille de la Résistance
4. Médaille Commemorative de la Guerre 1940-1945
   avec 2 éclairs entrecroises
5. Croix du Prisonnier Politique de la Guerre 1940-1945 avec 5 étoiles

I have the first two of them, but the whereabouts of the other three are unknown. The two I have were with Aunt Ghilly Godenne's belongings, but at the time of her passing no one knew exactly what they represented or who they honored. They easily could have belonged to Ghilly's father or grandfather which in fact is true of a few others found in the same box.

#8. I have the **complete file from the Belgian Archives** where honorary recognition is given to Isabelle Godenne from both Attorney Albert Melot (head of the Comet Line of Namur), and US Army Chief Marshall.

All these relics will eventually be turned over to our daughter, Jennifer O'Brien, for safe keeping, but also because she teaches history, as well as a course on genocides throughout history. She teaches at Ledyard High School in Ledyard, Connecticut. She is probably the best vehicle to pass this important story on to the younger generation, while keeping Tante Isa's memory and her heroism alive within our own families. This book will also help. The plan is to protect all the artifacts in some sort of glass museum-type cabinet.

*Croix de Chevalier de l'Ordre de Leopoldo II avec Palme...belonging to Tante Isa*

*left: L'Ordre de Leopold, Croix de Chevalier — maybe belonging to Tante Isa's brother, Pierre*
*Middle: Belgian - Croix de Guerre 1940 avec Palme ....belonging to Tante Isa*
*Right: WWI medal 1914-1918 maybe belonging to Tante Isa's brother, Pierre*

# Tante Isa's ALBUM: « Retour de Captivité »

*Tante Isa's return to Namur, Belgium from Waldheim Prison in Saxony, Germany*
*It took sixteen days: from May 9th to May 25th 1945.*

Her small, but beautiful album was accidently found in 2019 by John McCrea in his basement. It contains very little writing, but appears to be written by Tante Isa with the help of her niece Mary Godenne-McCrea-Curnen. There are several indicators that Mary was involved in putting together the album, the most significant is the photo of Tante Isa at the end of the album with the caption: "Ma Tante Isa" as if Mary was doing the writing.

The first page of this album records a list of 24 towns that the caravan of Allied army trucks went through as they returned the prisoners to their homes. You can trace her journey on the map. The album also contains a few post cards of Waldheim, and group photos of the other survivors. The groups seem to be organized by regions where they came from. They are being transported home in this military convoy, but the sense of freedom and elation is apparent. This is their D-Day, returning one town at a time.

*The list of towns (she misspelled a few.) is as follows*:

| | | |
|---|---|---|
| 1. | Waldheim Prison | Saxony, Germany |
| 2. | Gera | Thuringia, Germany |
| 3. | Iena/jena | Nuremberg, Germany |
| 4. | Weimar | Germany |
| 5. | Erfurt | Germany |
| 6. | Gotha | Germany |
| 7. | Eisenach | Germany |
| 8. | Bamberg | Germany |
| 9. | Sehweinfurt | Germany |
| 10. | Aschaffenburg | Germany |
| 11. | Hanau | Germany |
| 12. | Frankfort/Frankfurt | Germany |
| 13. | Mayence = Mainz | Germany |
| 14. | Kreuznach | Germany |
| 15. | Munster | Germany |
| 16. | Homburg | Germany |
| 17. | Saarebrucken/Saarbrucken | Germany (on the border with France) |
| 18. | Thionville | Lorraine, France |
| 19. | Bellembourg | Luxembourg |
| 20. | Luxembourg | Luxembourg |
| 21. | Longlier | Belgium |
| 22. | Neufchateau | Belgium |
| 23. | Dinant | Belgium |
| 24. | Namur | Belgium |

# LIFE AFTER LIBERATION

Like many of you, I have read lots of books about captivity during WWII in various different prison circumstances where the focus was always on survival and the resilience of the human spirit. However, I now realize that what happens afterward, if they live to be released and returned to what they remember as home, is just as challenging as their captivity. I do not as yet have any records of Tante Isa's thoughts or feelings the first few months or years after she came back to Namur. For example, I don't know if her mother passed away while she was in prison? I am fairly certain that her home and shop were intact. Her father was not alive when she was arrested. I believe her siblings were all still alive. I can say with certainty that the Tante Isa my sister, cousins, and I all met some twenty years after the war, was the kindest, warmest, caring individual you could imagine. She even had a wonderful sense of humor. Needless to say, she was also still a very devout Catholic. My intuition is that she would do it all over again.

Regarding the impact prison may have had on some, I am going to offer a few pages and excerpts from the biography: **A Train In Winter** *by Caroline Moorehead.* Moorehead was able to interview children of survivors and include information from memoires of prisoners regarding their return to post war homes that were drastically transformed both in terms of rubble, and missing or damaged family members. There existed a haunting emptiness, and the feeling that life would never be "normal" again.

**A Train In Winter:** *Chapter Fifteen: Slipping into the shadows (pg. 288-289)*

It was not long after Charlotte Delbo (a French prisoner) came home to Paris that she began to write about the German camps. Much of it was in verse.

> I've come back from another world,' she wrote,
> to this world
> I had not left
> and I know not
> which one is real...
> As far as I am concerned
> I'm still there
> dying there
> a little more each day
> dying over again
> the death of those who died...
> I have returned
> from a world beyond knowledge
> and now must unlearn
> for otherwise I clearly see
> I can no longer live.

Her words could have been written by any one of the 49 survivors out of the Convoy of 31,000 prisoners for each shared the same sense of alienation, loss and loneliness. In their two years and three months in the German camps they had been too cold, too frightened, too ill, too hungry, too dirty and too sad. They had witnessed both the worst and the best that life had to offer, cruelty, sadism, brutality, betrayal, thievery, but also generosity and selflessness. Their reserves of strength and character had been pushed to the very far limits of endurance and every notion of humanity had been challenged.

According to the author, Caroline Moorehead, an ambivalence marked them all. They no longer felt themselves to be the same people and, looking back at the young women they had once been, full of hope and confidence and excitement, they marveled at how innocent and trusting they had been. There was no innocence left, in any of them; and they would not find it again.

Having lived so intensely together, depending on each other to stay alive, they were now forced apart: by geography, by families, by a world whose rules and ways they had forgotten and which, physically weak, quickly exhausted, prematurely aged, they had to learn again. When, later, they met, they admitted to one another that the return to France in the early summer of 1945 had proved as hard and as unhappy as anything they had known. Return, they said, was a time of 'shadowy places, silences and things not said.'

(pg. 293)
What each of the survivors was now faced with was the question of how they would remake their lives, and how they would convey to their families what they had been through. Some had families and homes waiting for them but some did not, having been killed or destroyed by bombs.

Marie-Claude, an Auschwitz and Ravensbruck survivor had remarked, that her experiences were so extreme, so incomprehensible, so unfamiliar, that she, like the other women, doubted that they possessed the words to describe them, even if people wanted to hear; which, as it turned out, not many did.

(Taken from: **A Train in Winter**, by Caroline Moorehead)

## Obituary & Translation

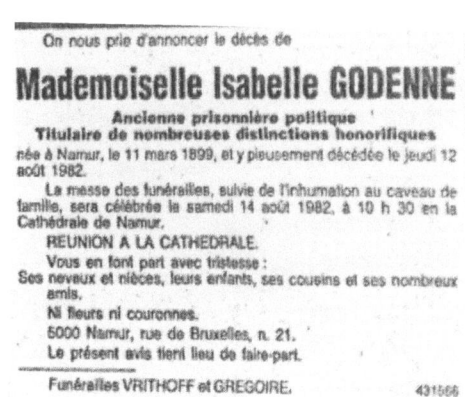 

*We regret to inform you of the passing of:*

### Mademoiselle Isabelle GODENNE

**Former political prisoner**
**Holder of numerous honorary distinctions**

born in Namur, March 11,1899 and piously died there Thursday August 12, 1982.

The funeral mass, followed by her burial in the family vault, will be celebrated on Saturday August 14, 1982 at 10:30 in the Cathedral of Namur.

### GATHERING AT THE CATHEDRAL

With sadness we invite you all to take part :
her nephews and nieces, their children, her cousins and her many friends.
No flowers or wreaths.
5000 Namur, street of Bruxelles, N. 21
Funeral Home Vrithoff and Gregoire

### THE RESISTANCE IS IN MOURNING

This Saturday in Namur was the funeral of Mlle. Isabelle Godenne, born on March 11,1899.

The late lamented prisoner, a member of an esteemed family from Namur specializing in the publishing and printing done during the last war, an active member of the Resistance in the "Zero Service" which played an important role.

Her patriotic activity caused her to be arrested by the occupying forces and to experience captivity in German camps. Recognized as a political prisoner, she received several awards of honorary distinction.

For all those who are impacted by her loss, family, friends, comrades in battle with Mlle. Godenne, our newspaper offers you its heartfelt condolences.

# FAMILY RECOLLECTIONS
Based on emails sent from my cousins and my sister

**Isabelle Burki (daughter of Jacques Godenne):** She mentioned that she knew Tante Isa was part of a Resistance network, possibly named Comete, and hoped to look through her father's papers for more information. (I, of course, wonder if both my cousins, Isabelle Burki and Isabelle Renard, are named after Tante Isa?)

**David Godenne (son of John/Jean Godenne):** He explained he had no idea Tante Isa took part in the Resistance. He said he had only met her a few times in his life, much after the war, and remembered her being very kind, but also severely diabetic. He recalls she was wonderful to his younger brother, Jerome, when he lived in Belgium. David further said how surprised he was to hear of Tante Isa's work with the Resistance because years later in conversations with Uncle Jacques about that dark period, he learned that Jacques' father, Pierre Godenne (Tante Isa's brother) asked Jacques not to participate in the actions of his patriotic comrades. (Born in 1921, Jacques would have been 18-24 during the German occupation.) David felt that Jacques suffered from his father's decree. David recalled that Uncle Jacques said he was "a frustrated, but obedient son, who was forbidden to risk his life in the Resistance", so he took up rock climbing.

**Andrew McCrea (son of Mary Godenne):** He thought that Tante Isa had a prison number tattooed on her arm. But that may not have been the case. He also remembers his mother, Mary, explaining that when Tante Isa was in prison (first St. Gilles Prison, then Forest Prison, both in Brussels before being transferred to Germany) her laundry was occasionally done by relatives. Cleverly, the desperate prisoners would write notes on tiny shreds of paper that were weaved into the socks they had knitted for themselves and passed with the laundry.

**Claire McCrea-Moore (daughter of Mary Godenne):** She also remembers this clandestine tactic that allowed the prisoners to communicate with the outside world. Claire recalls being told that Tante Isa was the only one who survived, but is not sure if this meant she was the only one in Namur, or of her Resistance group. Claire has proudly explained her middle name is Isabelle after Tante Isa. Lastly, Claire has mentioned that she still has a silk scarf from a downed pilot that she believes Tante Isa gave her. It has a map printed on it which was often how the Allied pilots carried such important information on their missions.

**Isabelle Renard (daughter of Elizabeth Godenne):** She sent me the obituary and death announcement, as well as a ten-page French transcript of Tante Isa's arrest, trial and sentencing. In this material, she states her belief that Tante Isa was an active member of the Resistance group called "Service Zero". This recorded information was extremely helpful and very different from the version I had from stories my mother had told me.

**Juliette Renard (daughter of Elizabeth Godenne):** She sent me still more information about the arrest and imprisonment of Tante Isa which included the mention of her first prison stay at St. Gilles and Forest Prisons in Brussels, her mother's typing of the file, dates of letters that were sent to and from Tante Isa. Also her mother, Elizabeth, found a suitcase in Tante Isa's attic with her prison uniform and file. She sent these items to the Center of Studies and Documentation of the Auschwitz Foundation which expressed their appreciation.

**Pierre McCrea (son of Mary Godenne):** He reminded us all about "Uncle André Suquet", who is maybe a cousin or very close friend to our grandfather, Pierre Godenne. My cousin thinks it was Uncle André who drove with the family south during the German advancement on Brussels. Later, Uncle André returned to Brussels a bit earlier than the others who had all been turned back at the border between France and Spain. He was asked to check if it was safe for the rest of the family to return to their home in Brussels, Belgium.

**Audrey Fay (daughter of Denyse Godenne):** She thinks that "Uncle André Suquet" was her godfather. He was married to Aunt Juliette. Audrey confirms they were very close to the Godenne family, although she is not sure of their exact relationship. Furthermore, as my sister, Audrey's recollections of Tante Isa are of course, very similar to mine.

# RESOURCES

1. Memories of discussions with my mother, Denyse Godenne/Skaggs
2. Memories of discussions with my Great Aunt Isabelle Godenne (Tante Isa)
3. Isabelle Renard   (my cousin in Belgium sent significant records)
4. Juliette Renard   (my cousin in Belgium sent important information)
5. Isabelle Burki    (my cousin in Switzerland, sent crucial material)
6. Shared memories, emails, comments, artifacts from all Godenne's
7. Fabrice.Maerten@arch.be          (Isabelle Godenne file : AA1333)
8. Cege Soma :  cegesoma@cegesoma.be  (Isabelle Godenne file : AA1333)
9. Quentin.Leroy@arch.be            (Isabelle Godenne file : AA1333)
10. archives@ville.namur.be   …no response
11. NARA – www.archives.gov (request: 5701226 series but closed due to Covid)
12. Staatsarchiv Leipzig – poststelle@sta.smi.sachsen.de  Waldheim Prison
13. Doreen.Wustig@sta.smi.sachsen.de     (Waldheim Prison, Isabelle Godenne)
14. "The Women in Waldheim Prison" by Gabriele Hacki
15. "A Train in Winter" by Caroline Moorehead
16. Gert.DEPRINS@arch.be (Isabelle Godenne, political prisoner :
    ref. PP 19032 Kal 1106)
        (her personal documentation file : d019578)
            … never responded with info or price to scan and send

www.ingramcontent.com/pod-product-compliance
Lightning Source LLC
LaVergne TN
LVHW072127070426
835512LV00002B/32